Timothy Prolific Veit Jones

Rebel Waters
Brooklyn, Long Island

Published by Rebel Waters Ink
Book Layout: Timothy Prolific Veit Jones

ISBN-13: 978-0-9779623-5-8
ISBN: 0-9779623-5-0
Library of Congress Control Number: 2017944930

Copyright © 2017 by Timothy William Veit Jones (Prolific).
All rights reserved. Printed in the United States of America. No part of this book or e-book may be used or reproduced, stored in a retrieval system or transmitted in any form or by any means electronic, mechanical, photocopying, recording or otherwise, without prior written permission except in the case of brief quotations embodied in critical articles or reviews. For information, please contact the publisher.

For booking & general inquiries, please contact
tim@projones.com

preface

Musaic details the fracturing of the patriarchal tendency to put women on pedestals and view them as fantastical creatures rather than entering into partnership with their humanity. In other words, many men (even well-intentioned ones) view women as objects – of affection, of pursuit, of sexual gratification.

It took a great deal of self-examination to understand how I've been guilty of objectifying women. Every woman I admired, dated, pursued, slept with, or entered a relationship with was a muse of my poetry at some point. In my youth, I sought and often found freedom in the embrace, among the hearts, and between the thighs of those I dated and/or loved. I learned more of who I was through them. However, they were not compensated for that mental, emotional, and spiritual labor. To all of the women that I've loved, lost, used, broken the hearts of, that have broken mine – I apologize. I never intended to make you sharecroppers of my personal development, but it happened. Even at my best, I know I fell short of who I needed to be and what I needed to give.

I wrote *Musaic* nearly a decade ago through a series of writing prompts with my cousin and frequent collaborator Cétáh Treadwell. In the years that followed, I declared myself a feminist because I learned that being an ally was no longer enough. Active participation in the liberation of femmes is as necessary as destroying white supremacy. The deconstruction of patriarchy is not the work of allyship, it is the work of an accomplice. Allies sympathize, observe, and join in the work when called. Accomplices are consistently present in the trenches.

Upon revisiting this book, I remembered the road to becoming an accomplice and the parts of myself I shed in order to do so. The earliest pieces of this book were written before my intentional journey toward a feminist practice. My sisters/mentors (Piper Anderson, Jennifer Cendaña Armas, Ella Turenne) introduced me to the existence of patriarchy, but I still saw myself as a "good guy." I resisted identifying with how my cis-hetero-male privilege supports the oppression of femme bodies.

Evolving and declaring myself a feminist does not absolve me of who I was, nor should it. If anything, it is proof that people can change when it is a priority. One day, I look forward to detailing what sparked this change in me, what caused me to believe that the urgency of deconstructing patriarchy is at times more important than defeating white supremacy. This is not that story.

This is a chronicle of the relationships that fell through my hands like grains of sand. It is a story of love, loss, heartbreak, imperfection, and the mourning of what could never be.

*Writers often fall in love with their muses.
Rarely is this a relationship that fares well.*

She steps out of a tornado
in a peach dress with black stilettos

We just met, but this feels
    like Songhai,
    like Tenochtitlan,
    like Maya,
    like the spark of creation,
    a first kiss,
    a fabled garden hanging in Babylon,
    a lost world wonder.

She makes pyramids cry sand.

She fits my grasp
    like a saxophone,
    like a bass, like a keyboard,
    fingers play, lips leak music,
    one glance melts me into lake.

Her walk: 44 magnum.
Smile: Hiroshima.

She makes my tongue hollow.
My way with words falls out.

Those eyes,
light brown,
burn like twin stars.

Their gravity attracting me was inevitable.

musaic

I.

This morning
a muse attempts suicide,
tired of giving the best of herself to men
who never give her credit.

These are not the days
when writers would tribute and invoke
beautiful voices to whisper
pyramids and cathedrals into ears.

Wind slices her flesh to bone.
Tendons & ligaments snap,

she doesn't
know if she
jumped
tripped
or if I
pushed

Lady Analog

You inspire fantasies of upside down kisses on playground swings.

Sophisticated Lady, ambient basketballs
in Ft. Greene parks pound out Ellington classics.
Traffic passes, horns blow Miles

Summertime swings chains Gillespie,
laughter Cannonball, every inch of your lips
drip into a chorus of Nina Simone records.
                                          Can I put a little sugar in your bowl?

I want to stay late,
spin the park between double-dutch ropes,
spend the day in time lapse photography.

                                          The Night Has a Thousand Eyes.
I want every one transfixed on you,
when you dance across constellations.

You are my *Equinox*,
the last real song I heard
before leaving Brooklyn to go home.

                           Bata drums beat beneath my epidermis.

I recall mornings I arose,
intoxicated by your scent,
dreaming of your touch.

The only time we kissed
was pressed lips to passed dutch.

II.

I place his fingertips in my wounds.

My imaginations tells me her lips taste like an apocalypse. She speaks, voice tumbling past moist smile, each word flickers. Lavender perfume whispers a strong potion. Arteries pulsate, fingertips tremble, usually sculpted words crumble in my mouth like withered clay. Standing behind her is like approaching an altar, proximity to sacred space makes hair stand on end.

Her voice raises ancestors in my veins.

III.

A disclaimer was tattooed to her ribcage:

You who would drink
inspiration from mutilated wrists

Morbi at leo.

Ingrese a su propio riesgo.

Entrez a vos risques et perlis.

Εισάγετε με δική σας ευθύνη.

Enter at your own risk.

My walls are crumbling
I am a civilization
past the straits of Gibraltar
weary of suffering
a pilgrimage here
would be unwise.

Tanka

Her paint and my words
sprawl a veduta across
pillow-top canvass.
Bodies pen haiku capable
of making Oshun blush.

Bathing in the Jordan

River currents pound my faults downstream.

I pray not to pollute you like the Ganges

with well-intended worship.

V.

A crown of thorns
dyes golden brown locks
a burgundy shade.

Wrists bleed profusely,
forearms bound to headboard.
Shoulder blades kiss,
love juice beads above hips.

Goosebumps punctuate nipples
ribcage stretches high, arched,
a proscenium above the stage of her passion

she moans anxiously, mango nectar slithers
down the inside of her thigh reminiscent of pomegranate
juice dripping from Eve's chin.

I enter, and the noon sun is eclipsed.

A final scream is exhaled.
The sheets are torn.

Rope falls from pinned ankles.

She walks off.

So do I.

V.

You knew better.

Thick skin splits cleanly, smelling of succulence and piety.

We burn like books under the legs of moors
fasting beneath a moon dulled.

Its splendor, victim of meteor and ice frigid,
a mausoleum of nights spent toe-tagging faith.

You cannot protect me.

VI.

Ventricles fracture,
shards quake in fear of sledgehammer
words and brass knuckle reality.

Syllables pull cardiac tissue wishbone.
She snaps me with one kiss.

I taste mortality.

Her tongue is a mirror casting a reflection I refuse to face.
She speaks my failures in a voice that crumbles the world I know.
Sentences cut the cords of lies I've told her and myself.

I lie about simple things. Stupid things.

Arguments stain brick walls crimson.

Mosaic

Fragments of my heart are scattered
in every woman I have ever loved.

The muscle is a bombed church.

Damage came from within
as much as it did from without.

*Fragments of your heart are scattered
in every woman you've ever loved?*

*Why don't you go back, collect them,
mortar, jagged edges,
build a cathedral of self pity,
you sucker for love ass nigga.*

Crux Immissa

I.

Her kisses are the sweetest arsenic.

Loving her is a crown of thorns
a slow asphyxiation
each touch nailed me
knees broken as i hung
"Forgive her Father…"

It is Done.

II.

Two crisp $20 bills cut the air as they landed in my lap.
The cost of mobility is shackling you to a monotonous existence.

You are not a homebody.
This isn't home for you
No matter how much I want it to be.

I can only help with things I can control.
$40 ain't shit, but it was given freely.
Freely in an effort to cover the cost to get out
during the days I spend at work.
My way of saying let me help.

To your hand it was highway litter.

It may as well have been a palm swung.
My face is less tender than my pride.

VII.

*You fancy yourself a demigod
wrapped in my thighs,
heroic ego wide with romantic
notions of love's immortality.*

VIII.

I depart, exhausted from bandaging her slit writs daily.
I was never instructed how to mend self-mutilation.

She cannot stomach my heart.
I found it regurgitated in a trash can
behind the skeletons in her closet.

9.9.9.

I want to curse
this beating muscle
in my chest

that drums 808s for you,
but I love music.

A woman of your quality
should make any man strip naked,
cool discarded like python skin,
the kind that could unfork a tongue,
and propel fallen angels back into heaven.

Our nights proved my mortality.

I witnessed continental drift first hand.
Plateaus of possibility were carved into canyons of silence.
Never have these eyes witnessed a star extinguish.

When you spoke, I quaked before a shrub on fire that would not burn.

Record of your voice has faded.

These fingers that once clasped yours
and stroked your hair
trace your image daily.

Every drawing of you hooks into words.

If this were written in Arabic,
maybe the letters would resemble your irises.

Decrescendo

For everything I said
the things I have not
actions mismatched
intentions unmet
accidental narci
ssism lack of
considera
tion, thes
e things
erode
wha
t m
at
e
r
s.

Solitary sidewalk jaunts
reflect memories like headlights
on moist pavement.

There is space under my umbrella for two.
Her heels clicked off against asphalt
long ago. Stilettos hit the road.

High beam eyes burn my retinas,
radial imprint lasts for weeks.
I still see her carved inside my eyelids.

This is the end of a different journey.

Adjust your approach and find your way
find your way back to the center

or

take the journey in reverse.

Day 40

Deferred dreams swing in lynched body metronome,
sing lullabies of cracked ribs,
a sweet chariot destined to open arteries.

carry me home.

Fear of failure binds me.
I will not till the soil of others' dreams
at the expense of my soul.

I had as many arms as Shiva,
each palm laid flat against my chest
held me back.

I am shackled by the inability
to acknowledge my inner divinity.

I am
a confined Krishna,
a clandestine Christ,
a breaking wave crest in an ocean of God
attempting to recognize his face.

Day 36

My fingers knew how to make her speak Joplin and Chopin
each finger stroking chords that made wood

writhe in ecstasy. She was an older lover who taught me
the affects of neglect. I tired of entering her for hours,
discarding her for younger pursuits with colorful buttons.

This house stopped being a home a long time ago.

I ignored her as I sat ten feet away and wrote my first poem.

Day 35

70 years of memories are etched into discolored chipped ivory.

It sits in his house as the product of divorce

I begged my great-aunt Marjorie for the instrument.
It sits in my father's living room, covered in dust,
keys as out of tune as my ability to read music.

The bench is stained with discarded words
memories from a childhood disavowed

The secrets it keeps make it too heavy to transport to an apartment.

I wear braggadocio and swagger like my Sunday best,
tailored to fit a character that remains played off stage.
Most days, I'd rather be on a mountain meditating somewhere.

I fear of what will happen when still my mind.
I've felt my psyche crack. Maybe I should have myself committed.

I'm a man.

Men don't speak these thoughts out loud,
don't ask for help or shed tears.
We bleed and shed blood. Or so I'm told.

I'm a man.

Day 30

Being in church every Sunday was a charade.
I learned to walk, insulate, and forget. It taught me
the art of smiling through broken ribs.

It's not the church's fault that I absorbed the wrong lessons.
Maybe it's the adults' fault for teaching them.
Maybe it's my fault for straying.

I've carried this habit into adulthood.
I appear to have everything together
while I'm actually on the brink of insanity.

I'm not insane, nor on the brink. Failure
is a bitter pill coated with self-pity, a reminder
that coats stomach with bile and blood.

I'm perceived as confident, smart, and articulate.
I often think the opposite. I despise my own reflection,

wondering if a touch of my finger could boil holy water,
extinguish candles, make the pews rise in protest to my presence.

What kind of forgiveness is there for a fallen angel?
I'm not an angel, pristine, winged, righteous, or fallen.

I'm a man.

Day 25

I have hatchets to bury.

Napalm drenched words decorate ornate pyramids with limbs.
Their spirits visit me daily as I sharpen my tongue.
I have navigated fields soaked with the blood of consequence.

A feathered tomahawk attached to my belt
drags across my soul, an anchor impeding
my vessel from leaving port.

I will not let hate rob me of heaven.
Carrying this any longer
will break my wings.

I want to forgive family.

Day 20

Find me a redemption song
whose lyrics and the parchment they are printed on
are not tainted.

Find me a flag to fly
that doesn't resemble prison bars,
bloodstained cotton, and the complexion of those
it was not woven to represent.

Find me a reason to feel American today
that doesn't involve murder.

Day 19

Burial grounds are desecrated
with new skyscrapers.

Basements are tombs,
streets and avenues
cemetery roads,
pavement concealing
piles of lost bones.

Day 18

Sacrifice makes this city fertile.
Battery City Parking is unlikely sacred ground.

The Tribute of Light
is installed on a garage roof,
not in hallowed stone footprints.

He asked me to
confess my sins. I asked
him to wash his hands.

Holy water parted his flesh.
Skeletal remains pointed
toward the nearest exit.

I decided that
this church was no more holy
than the Capitol.

Day 11

I have witnessed
bright futures scourged at the foot
of a local Golgotha.

In need of hope, I
speedily walked to the
closest church in town.

This morning I left
the third pew nauseated.
Pastor is a fiend.

He was caught smoking
offerings in a crack pipe,
inhaling distilled
prayers, selling illusion.

Before the altar
boy he turned his rod into
a writhing serpent.

He told the woman
that kneeling was the gateway
to absolution.

There never has been
another pimp so revered
by good bougie folk.

Day 10

Neglecting to worship at this temple
left stale prayers on the altar rotting
under a heap of incense ash.

A candle burns soft, flickers through frosted red glass
like abandoned memories. Marble floors carry
faint echoes of sung praises.

Abandoned pews fracture, Arches breathe heavily,
lungs reek with the scent of blood.

Eli, Eli, lama sabachthani?*

*My God, my God, why have You forsaken me?

until I realize that it can't be
made with real cheese for $1.

There is no way this shit is healthy.

When did Mamoun's falafel become $3.50?
When did I become so broke that I can't afford falafel?
Being 30 is supposed to be less broke than being 20

but here I am a broke college student again
working a full-time job that still sustain bills that ain't even in my name.
A taste for expensive bourbon doesn't help.

I'm usually all Deepak Chopra - present in the motherfucking moment,
contemplating my role in the world, but I'm too hungry
to focus on anything other than this $1 slice of shit.

Fuck it, I'm buying two. The homeless
guy standing outside is waaaay hungrier than me, and I
live in the suburbs. Who the fuck am I to complain?

Day 7

The fridge has half a loaf of bread
a quarter of an onion, two tomatoes
one green pepper, three pitchers

of filtered water, curry tuna salad,
five eggs, four slices of american cheese,
two pieces of frozen chicken,

half a bag of potatoes I hope ain't rotten,
a pot of three day old vegetarian curry,
and a small tupperware of beef chilli.

Pocket has $3, bank account is -$30,
best dress shoes have a hole in the sole
from walking 3 miles home from the railroad

cost of a cab is $10, I have $3
cost of an unlimited metrocard is $106,
I have $3. Walk to work walk to school

walk home walk to grocery store
no money for public transportation.
Good thing I know how to hop turnstiles.

No free lunch at work today,
boss is on vacation, $3 in my pocket.
I think $1 pizza is worth it…

Day 2

the night sings a lullaby of switchblades
wrist arteries surround time-bomb sinew

which do I cut to diffuse?

red wire
blue wire

fire.

Day 1

threat of foreclosure
tastes shotgun

barrel presses lips like hand rolled cigars
smoke fills cheeks buckshot

dances with back of throat before it exhales
thoughts across plaster

shell casings line stomach
gunpowder drowned in whiskey

bile Pollacks pavement
red-yellow holes in concrete
glow brightly in damp dusk air

swallow hard

Welcome to a desert where the sun plays Russian roulette, a place where a fresh bullet's trajectory blocked by an empty shell in the chamber is all that will save you from yourself.

A place for prayer with no certainty of an answer, even if you are God.

A place where mirages and idols beckon, and the mind attempts to discern between the divine and the devilish, a wasteland staircase of psalms, a mountain that speaks in wind and thunder.

For anyone who ever needed to write their way out.

40 Days, 40 Nights: A Lullaby of Shotguns and Switchblades

Published by Rebel Waters Ink

Book Layout: Timothy Prolific Veit Jones

ISBN-13: 978-0-9779623-5-8

ISBN: 0-9779623-5-0

Library of Congress Control Number: Pending

Copyright © 2017 by Timothy William Veit Jones (Prolific).

All rights reserved. Printed in the United States of America. No part of this book or e-book may be used or reproduced, stored in a retrieval system or transmitted in any form or by any means electronic, mechanical, photocopying, recording or otherwise, without prior written permission except in the case of brief quotations embodied in critical articles or reviews. For information, please contact the publisher.

For booking & general inquiries, please contact

tim@projones.com

Timothy Prolific Veit Jones

Rebel Waters
Brooklyn, Long Island

www.ingramcontent.com/pod-product-compliance
Lightning Source LLC
Chambersburg PA
CBHW052030290426
44112CB00014B/2458